THE FLAG OF THE UNITED KIN GREAT BRITAIN AND NORTHERN IRELAND

THE UNION JACK

THE POCKET BOOK
OF BRITISH PATRIOTISM

Compiled by George Courtauld

'This story shall the good man teach his son'

For my boys with all my love

STERLING PUBLISHING
New York

Published by Sterling Publishing Co., Inc.
387 Park Avenue South, New York, NY 10016

© 2004 by Halstead Books, Ltd.

Distributed in Canada by Sterling Publishing
c/o Canadian Manda Group, 165 Dufferin Street
Toronto, Ontario, Canada M6K 3H6

ISBN: 1-4027-2835-2

Library of Congress Cataloging-in-Publication Data available upon request.

1 3 5 7 9 8 6 4 2

Manufactured in Mexico

INTRODUCTION

I am a married forty-year-old father of three boys under twelve. I live in the English countryside and have commuted to London by train for the last fourteen years. My wife is a nurse, working locally in the public health service.

Last year on Christmas Eve, I was taking the train home for the holidays. Six angelic children, charming, smiling, and polite, boarded the train and sat in a huddle singing carols. One boy, who had his arm in a sling, was unable to sit with the rest. A kindly older woman offered to swap seats with him, suggesting that little Lord Nelson might like to sit with his friends.

The boy looked confused. "Nelson!" the woman insisted. "England expects? Admiral Nelson?"

"Oh, of course!" the young boy exclaimed. "That guy from *Star Trek*!"

Saddened and amazed, I recounted the story to my wife and children when I got home, only to be shown up myself when my eldest son asked me when the Cross of St. George had become our national flag.

"Certainly some time after we became Christian," I blustered.

"Was that before or after Muhammad?" another son inquired.

I decided there and then that I needed to put something together for all of us.

Over the Christmas holiday I researched and wrote a short history chart containing everything I thought my children ought to know about British history.

News of my history chart spread among friends and family and within two months over a hundred people had asked me for a photocopy. I soon realized there was a massive demand for a simple British history book. I spent the next six months researching and expanding my timeline, and *The Pocket Book of Patriotism* was born.

Over the following summer, I managed to persuade representatives of seven British publishing houses to meet me, in the hope that one of them might publish the book. I was rejected out of hand by all seven. All felt that the use of the word "patriotism" in the title was at the very best distasteful, if not downright offensive. Three senior publishing executives even assured me that patriotism was an obsolete concept. I then resolved to publish the book myself.

At the end of October I instructed a printer to produce ten thousand books, and on Thursday morning, November 18, the first two thousand copies rolled off the presses. By Monday we had sold 2500 copies; by the following Thursday, articles began to appear in the national press, including *The Daily Telegraph, The Sunday Times,* and *The Daily Mail;* and by Christmas Eve, exactly one year from the Lord Nelson conversation on the train, we had sold 140,000 books.

Due to all the letters, calls, and encouragement from American friends and relations who managed to get *The Pocket Book of Patriotism* sent over from London, I am thrilled that it will now be available in the USA. My great-great-great-grandfather, also a George Courtauld, was so enamored of the United States that he added Washington to his name, emigrated to the United States, and was ultimately buried in Pittsburgh in 1823. I would be immensely gratified and proud if the *The Pocket Book of Patriotism* could contribute in any way to the long-standing and mutual Anglo-American love and respect.

GEORGE COURTAULD, **London, January 2005**

BRITAIN	_ABROAD_
	_c 2550 BC_ The Great Pyramid of Khufu
_2200 BC–1300 BC_ Stonehenge	_c 1750 BC_ The Babylonian Eye for an Eye law
	_c 1250 BC_ The Trojan War
	_c 1225 BC_ Moses given the Ten Commandments
	_970 BC_ The death of King Solomon of Israel
_800 BC_ The Celts arrive in Britain	
	_776 BC_ The first Olympic Games
	_753 BC_ Rome founded by Romulus & Remus
	_563–483 BC_ The life of Buddha
	_551–479 BC_ The life of Confucius
	_490 BC_ The Greek victory over the Persians at Marathon
	_430–404 BC_ Athens fights Sparta in The Peloponnesian War
	_399 BC_ Socrates commits suicide
	_384–332 BC_ The life of Aristotle
	_356–323 BC_ The life of Alexander the Great
	_264–146 BC_ The Punic Wars between Rome & Carthage
_250 BC_ The first Hill Forts	
	_218 BC_ Hannibal leads his army over the Alps
	_214 BC_ The Great Wall of China completed
	_206 BC–AD 220_ The Han Dynasty, China
_55 BC_ Julius Caesar's first Invasion of Britain	
	_44 BC_ Caesar murdered
	_27 BC–14 AD_ Octavian (Augustus) becomes the first Emperor of Rome
	_3 BC_ The Birth of Jesus:

"I am the way, the truth and the life."

BRITAIN	ABROAD
	30 AD Jesus Crucified
43 The Roman Invasion and Conquest of Britain	
47 The Fosse Way completed	
50 London founded	
61 Boadicea leads the Iceni in revolt against the Romans	
	64 Rome burnt and Christians persecuted under Emperor Nero
70–84 The Roman Conquest of Wales & the North	
	79 The eruption of Mt Vesuvius destroys Pompeii
	80 The Colosseum of Rome completed
84 The Battle of Mons Graupius, Roman victory over the Caledonians:	

"To plunder, butcher, steal, these things they misname Empire:
They make a desolation and they call it peace."

	105 Paper invented in China
122 Work starts on Hadrian's wall	
	135 The Romans take Jerusalem
	c 300 The Stirrup invented
306 Constantine the Great declared Emperor at York	
304 The death of St Alban: the first Christian martyred in Britain	
	330 Constantine founds Constantinople
	397 The 'Confessions' of Saint Augustine
	400 The British Monk Pelagius denies the importance of Original Sin
409 The Roman Legions abandon Britain	
	410 Rome is sacked by the Visigoths

BRITAIN	ABROAD

c 446 The British make their final plea for help from Rome :

"To Aetius, thrice consul, the groans of the Britons. The barbarians push us to the sea, the sea pushes us back on the barbarians.Between these two kinds of death we are either drowned or slaughtered."

450–750 Britain is settled by the Angles, Saxons and Jutes, and evolves into the Seven Kingdoms of Northumbria, Mercia, Wessex, Essex, Sussex, Kent and East Anglia
450 Kent is settled by the Saxons Hengist & Horsa

453 The death of Attila the Hun

455 The Saxon Hengist turns on the British Vortigern
455 Rome is sacked by The Vandals
460 St Patrick returns to convert Ireland

469 The Visigoths invade Spain

510 The Battle of Mount Badon: British victory over the Saxons

529 The Benedictines founded
537 The Haghia Sophia of Constantinople finished

563 St Columba established on Iona
570–80 The Anglo Saxons consolidate their hold on the British Lowlands

"Not Angles, but Angels." Pope Gregory on seeing Angle slaves

597 St Augustine reaches Britain renewing contact with Rome

619–906 The Tang Dynasty, China
625 Mohammed starts reciting the Koran

664 The Synod of Whitby favours Roman over Celtic Christianity
673–735 The life of the Venerable Bede, the "Father of English History"

Britain	*Abroad*

Britain	Abroad
	674 The Arabs attack Constantinople
698 The Lindisfarne Gospels	
	711 The Arabs reach Spain
750 'Beowulf'	*751* The Buddhist 'Diamond Sutra': The first printed book
757–96 King Offa rules Saxon Mercia	
	788 Work starts on The Great Mosque at Cordoba
789 Offa's Dyke constructed	
793 The Vikings begin raiding Britain:	

"Behold the church of St Cuthbert, spattered with the blood
of the priests of God."

Britain	Abroad
800 'The Book of Kells'	*800* Charlemagne of France crowned Holy Roman Emperor
866–77 Invasion of the Great Danish (or Viking) Army	
867 The Danes take Northumbria	
870 St Edmund murdered	*870* Gunpowder invented in China
871 The Battle of Ashdown: The Saxons defeat the Danes	

The Reign of Alfred the Great, King of Wessex
871 – 99

Britain	Abroad
886 The North subjected to the Danelaw, the rule of the Danes	
889 The Anglo Saxon Chronicle starts	*889* Angkor founded
900–50 Conquest of the Danelaw	
	910 The Benedictine Abbey at Cluny founded
	911 Rollo the Viking hailed as the first Duke of Normandy
	933 Delhi founded

The Reign of Edgar
959 – 75

"Edgar the Glorious, by the Grace of Christ illustrious King of the English."

962 Otto I becomes Holy Roman Emperor

973 The British Princes acknowledge King Edgar as their overlord

The Reign of Aethelred the Unready
978 – 1016

Resumption of Danish Invasions

987 Hugh Capet crowned in France

991 The Battle of Maldon:
Viking victory over Saxons
991 Danegeld first extorted

992 Venice & Byzantium make their first formal trading agreement

The Reign of Canute the Dane
1016 – 35

1018 King Canute also becomes King of Denmark

1035 William, the future Conqueror, proclaimed Duke of Normandy

The Reign of Edward the Confessor, restoring the line of Wessex
1042 –1066

1054 Eastern & W. Churches split
1055 The Seljuk Turks reach Baghdad

1065 Westminster Abbey completed

The Reign of Harold II
1066

1066 The Battle of Stamford Bridge:
Saxon victory over invading Vikings

1066 The Battle of Hastings: The invading Normans defeat the Saxons

THE NORMANS
The Reign of William I, The Conqueror
1066 – 87

1070 Work starts on Canterbury Cathedral
1071 Hereward the Wake holds the Isle of Ely

1071 The Seljuk Turks take Jerusalem

1074 The Bayeux Tapestry

1078 Work starts on The Tower of London

1085 The Moors ejected from Toledo

1086 The Domesday Book

"There was no single hide nor indeed was one ox, one cow or one pig ... not put down in his record."

The Reign of William II, Rufus The Redhead
1087 – 1100

1094 El Cid takes Valencia
1096–1099 The First Crusade

The Reign of Henry I, Beauclerk
1100 – 35

The Curia Regis, forerunner of Parliament

1100 The Ceremony of Marriage to the Sea first performed in Venice
1116 Bologna University founded
1118 The Knights Templar established

1120 The loss of the White Ship
1131 The Abbeys of Tintern, Rievaulx & Fountains established

The Reign of King Stephen,
contesting control with his cousin Empress Matilda
1135 – 54

"Nineteen long winters when God and his Angels slept."

1139–1153 Civil War: 'The Anarchy'

1141 King Stephen a prisoner

1135 Flying buttresses appear in France

1140 Arabic numerals adopted in the West

1147–1149 The Second Crusade

THE PLANTAGENETS

The Reign of Henry II
1154 – 89

Trial by Jury becomes more common place
The Cross of St. George established as the national flag
1154 Work starts on York Minster

1155 Frederick of Barbarossa proclaimed Holy Roman Emperor
1155 Pope Adrian IV, (Nicholas Breakspear, the only English Pope,) grants Ireland to Henry II of England
1163 Work starts on Notre Dame

1169–70 Richard de Clare, Strongbow, begins the conquest of Ireland
1170 Thomas Beckett, the Archbishop of Canterbury, murdered:

"Will no one rid me of this turbulent Priest!" King Henry

1174 Work starts on Wells Cathedral

1174 Leaning Tower of Pisa built
1187 Saladin captures Jerusalem

The Reign of Richard I, The Lion Heart
1189 – 99

1190–94 King Richard on Crusade

1193 King Richard a prisoner in
Austria

1190 The Teutonic Knights established
1190 The Third Crusade
1192 Yoromito Minamoto proclaimed
Shogun of Japan

"The Devil is out. Look to yourself."

The King of France to John, on learning of King Richard's release.

1195–1199 King Richard at war in
France

1194 Chartres Cathedral begun

The Reign of King John, Lackland, Softsword
1199 – 1216

1204 The Loss of Normandy

1208–1214 The Pope imposes an
Interdict on England
1209 The Pope excommunicates
King John

1200 The University of Paris founded
1201 The Fourth Crusade
1204 Constantinople sacked by the
Crusaders
1208–1214 The Albigensian Crusade

1210 China invaded by Genghis Khan
1210 The Franciscans founded by St
Francis of Assisi
1212 The Childreńs Crusade

1214 The Battle of Bouvines: King
John loses empire in France
1215 Civil War
1215 King John forced to sign the
Magna Carta:

1215 The Dominicans founded

"To no man will we sell, or deny, or delay right or justice."

The Reign of Henry III 1216 – 72

1220 Work starts on Salisbury
Cathedral
1221–1224 Dominicans & Franciscans
arrive in England

1222 The University of Padua
founded
1224 Genghis Khan leads his
Mongols into Europe
1232 The first military use of rockets
in China
1234 The Chin dynasty brought
down by the Mongols

1240 The death of Llewellyn I ap
Gruffydd of Wales

1248 Seville captured from the
Moors by Ferdinand of Castile
1250–1570 The Marmelukes rule
Egypt

1249 University College, the first
Oxford College, founded
1258 The Provisions of Oxford: The
Barons take charge of royal
Government

1260 Kubla Khan becomes Emperor
of Mongolia

1264 The Battle of Lewes: Simon de
Montfort, the self styled 'Steward of
England', captures King Henry
1265 The Battle of Evesham and death
of de Montfort:

"God have mercy on our souls for our bodies are theirs."

1267 Roger Bacon's 'Opus Maius'

1267 Thomas Aquinas's 'Summa
Theologiae'

The Reign of Edward I, Longshanks, The Hammer of the Scots
1272 – 1307

1281 Peterhouse, the first Cambridge College founded
1281 The death of Llewellyn II ap Gruffydd of Wales
1282–1283 King Edward conquers Wales

1288–1919 The Ottomans assume power in Turkey

1290 The Expulsion of the Jews from England
1296 King Edward invades Scotland and takes the Stone of Destiny from Scone to Westminster
1297 The Battle of Stirling Bridge: The Scots under William Wallace defeat the English
1298 The Battle of Falkirk. King Edward defeats Wallace
c 1300 The Longbow invented
1301 King Edward invests his heir as the Prince of Wales
1306 The Rebellion of Robert The Bruce

c 1300 Gunpowder reaches the West

1306 The Expulsion of the Jews from France

The Reign of Edward II
1307 – 27

1307 Dante's 'Divine Comedy'
1309 The Pope leaves Rome and goes to Avignon

1314 The Battle of Bannockburn: The Scots defeat the English
1320 The Scots make the Declaration of Arbroath
"It is in truth not for glory nor riches nor honours that we are fighting but for freedom—for that alone which no honest man gives up but with life itself."

BRITAIN	ABROAD
1321–22 Civil War	
	1325 The Aztecs come to power in Mexico
1326–7 Overthrow and murder of King Edward by Queen Isabella and Mortimer	

The Reign of Edward III
1327 – 77

"The affairs that concern the King and the estate of his realm shall be directed by the common counsel of his realm and in no other wise."

	1334 Work starts on Giotto's Campanile in Florence, 'Giotto's Tower'
1337 King Edward claims the throne of France	
1337 The 100 Years War begins with the Invasion of France	
1340 The Battle of Sluys: Victory over the French at sea	
1346 The Battle of Crecy: Victory over the French:	

"Let the boy win his spurs." King Edward of his son, the Black Prince

1346 The Battle of Neville's Cross: Victory over the Scots	
1347 Calais falls to the English	
1348 The Black Death	
1350 'Sir Gawain & the Green Knight'	
1351 The Statute of Labourers	
1356 The Battle of Poitiers: The English capture King Jean II of France	*1356* The Ottoman Turks attack Europe

BRITAIN	*ABROAD*

1360 The Peace of Bretigny:
Aquitaine surrendered to England
King Edward renounces his claim to
Normandy
1362 Parliament is opened in
English which also replaces French
in the Courts

1366 Petrarch's Sonnets
1368–1644 The Ming Dynasty, China

1369 France retakes Aquitaine,
renewing hostilities
1370 The Black Prince, 'The comfort
of England', sacks Limoges
1376 The Good Parliament: Elects a
'Speaker' for the first time and urges
the King to:

"Live off his own."

1376 The death of the Black Prince:

"Such as thou art, so once was I. As I am now, so thou wilt be."

The Reign of Richard II
1377 – 99

1377 The Pope returns to Rome

1377 John Wyclif, 'The Morning Star
of the Reformation', preaches
against the Pope, monks and friars,
attracting followers to the Lollard
movement
1380 John Wyclif translates the Bible

1378–1415 The Great Schism: Rival
Popes at Avignon and Rome

1381 The Peasants Revolt:

"When Adam delved and Eve span who then was the gentleman?"
John Ball

"You shall have no other Captain but I."
King Richard fearlessly riding into the mob of hostile 'Peasants'
after their leader, Wat Tyler, had been cut down by Richard's men

1385 The Visconti assume power in Milan

1387 Chaucer's 'Canterbury Tales'

1393 The Ottoman Turks take Bulgaria
1395 The Golden Horde defeated by Tamberlane

1396 The Peace of Paris: England retains only Calais and part of Gascony

THE HOUSE OF LANCASTER

The Reign of Henry IV
1399 – 1413

1400 The Rebellion of Owain Glyndwr
1403 Defeat and Death of Henry Percy, Hotspur, at Shrewsbury

1408 Donatello's 'David'

Reign of Henry V
1413 – 22

1415 The Battle of Agincourt: Victory over the French:

"Cry 'God for Harry! England and St George!'"

1419 The Fall of Rouen to the English
1420 The Treaty of Troyes recognises King Henry as heir to the French crown

1420 The Portuguese under Prince Henry the Navigator start exploring West Africa

Reign of Henry VI
1422 – 61

1423/4 The English victories at
Cravant and Verneuil
1428 The English beseige Orleans
1429 Joan of Arc relieves Orleans
1430 Joan of Arc burnt at the stake

1430's Van Eyck refines the art of
painting in oil.
1434 The Medicis assume power in
Florence
1436 The French recapture Paris from
the English

1440 Eton College founded
1444 The Treaty of Tours. Five year
truce
1450 John Cade's rebellion
1453 The End of the 100 Years War:
England retains only Calais

1453 The Ottoman Turks take
Constantinople.
1454 Movable type used by Gutenberg

1455 The Battle of St. Albans:
The start of the Wars of the Roses
1461 The Battle of Towton:
King Henry deposed

THE HOUSE OF YORK

The Reign of Edward IV
1461 – 83

1469 Spain united by the marriage of
Ferdinand of Aragon and Isabella of
Castile

1469 Malory's 'Morte d'Arthur':

"Whoso pulleth out this sword of this stone and anvil is
rightwise King born of all England."

Britain	Abroad
1471 Warwick the Kingmaker killed at Barnet **1474** William Caxton produces the first printed book in English	
	1479 The Spanish Inquisition established

Reign of Edward V
One of the murdered 'Princes in the Tower'
1483

Reign of Richard III
1483 – 5

| **1485** The Battle of Bosworth: Defeat and death of King Richard | |

THE HOUSE OF TUDOR

The Reign of Henry VII
1485 – 1509

1487 The Rebellion of Lambert Simnel	**1487** Diaz rounds the Cape of Good Hope **1492** Christopher Columbus reaches the West Indies **1497** Leonardo's 'Last Supper' **1498** Vasco da Gama reaches Calicut, India
1499 John Cabot reaches Newfoundland	
	1503 Leonardo's 'Mona Lisa' **1508** Michaelangelo starts work on the ceiling of the Sistine Chapel

Reign of Henry VIII
1509 – 47

	1509 Erasmus's 'In praise of folly'
1513 War with France and Scotland	
1513 The Battle of Flodden: Victory over the Scots	
1516 Thomas More's 'Utopia'	*1516* Macchiavelli's 'The Prince'
	1517 Luther publishes his 95 Theses
	1518 Titian, 'the father of modern painting' completes 'The Assumption'
	1519 Hernando Cortés leads his Spaniards into Mexico
1520 The Field of the Cloth of Gold	
1521 King Henry made Fidei Defensor (Defender of the Faith)	*1521* The end of the Aztec Empire
	1521 The Diet of Worms: The start of the Reformation
1526 William Tyndale's English translation of the New Testament	
1527 King Henry decides on divorce	*1527* Rome sacked
	1529 The Ottoman Turks attack Vienna
1529 The Fall of Cardinal Wolsey:	

"Had I but served God as diligently as I have served the King,
he would not have given me over in my grey hairs."

1533 King Henry marries Anne Boleyn	*1533* The end of the Inca Empire
1534 The Act of Supremacy: The Pope's authority in England abolished	*1534* The Jesuits, the Society of Jesus, founded
1535 The executions of More & Fisher	*1535* Cartier reaches the St Lawrence River
1536 Anne Boleyn executed	
1536 The Pilgrimage of Grace	*1536* Calvin in Geneva
1536 The Dissolution of the Monasteries	

1536 Wales becomes part of political
Union with England
1538 Holbein's 'Anne of Cleves'
1540 The Execution of Thomas
Cromwell
1542 The Battle of Solway Moss:
Victory over the Scots

1543 Copernicus's 'DeRevolutionibus

The Reign of Edward VI
1547 – 53

1547-9 Somerset's Protectorate

1547 Robert Ket's Rebellion:

1547 Ivan the Terrible of Russia
adopts the title Tsar

"He hath conceived a wonderful hate against all gentlemen."

1549 The First Book of Common
Prayer

The Reign of Mary I, Bloody Mary
1553 – 8

1554 The Execution of Lady Jane Grey
1554 Wyatt's rebellion
1554–6 England reunited with Rome
1555 Latimer & Ridley burnt at the
stake:

"Be of good comfort, Master Ridley, and play the man.
We shall this day light such a candle by God's Grace in England,
as I trust shall never be put out."
Hugh Latimer

1556 Cranmer burnt at the stake

1556–1605 Akbar the Great rules
India

1558 The Loss of Calais:
"When I am dead and opened you shall find 'Calais' lying in my heart."
Queen Mary

The Reign of Elizabeth I
1558 – 1603

"This is the Lord's doing and it is marvellous in our eyes."
Psalm 118 **Queen Elizabeth**

1563 The Thirty Nine Articles
1563 Foxe's Book of Martyrs
1565 Sir Walter Raleigh introduces tobacco and potatoes
1568 Mary Queen of Scots flees to England

1570 Palladio's 'Four Books of Architecture'

1570 Queen Elizabeth excommunicated:

"I would not open windows into men's souls."

1570 Leonard Digges invents the theodolite

1571 The Battle of Lepanto ends the Turkish threat to Europe from the sea
1572 The St Bartholomew's Day Massacre

1577–80 Drake's first voyage round the world

1584 Virginia established by Sir Walter Raleigh

1587 Mary Stuart, Queen of Scots, executed
1587 Drake's raid on Cadiz:

"I have singed the Spanish King's beard."

1588 The defeat of the Spanish
Armada:

"There is plenty of time to win this game and thrash the Spaniards too."
Drake's response to the sighting of the Armada during a game of bowls

"I know I have the body of a weak and feeble woman,
but I have the heart and stomach of a King, and a King of England too!"
Queen Elizabeth to her troops at Tilbury

1590 Spencer's 'Faerie Queene',
Marlow's 'Tamburlaine the Great'
1594 Shakespeare's 'Romeo & Juliet'
1598 Shakespeare's 'Henry V'   1598 The Edict of Nantes grants
                                        tolerance to French Protestants
1600 The East India Company
founded
1601 Essex's Rebellion

"Though God hath raised me high, yet this I count the glory of my crown:
that I have reigned with your loves." **Queen Elizabeth**

1601 Shakespeare's 'Hamlet'
1603 The death of Queen Elizabeth:

"All my possessions for a moment of time." Her last words

THE HOUSE OF STUART

The Reign of James I (VI of Scotland)
1603 – 25

"The state of Monarchy is the supremest thing upon earth;
… even by God himself they (Kings) are called Gods." **King James**

                                        1605 Cervantes 'Don Quixote'
1605 The Gunpowder Plot:
    "A desperate disease requires a dangerous remedy." **Guy Fawkes**

BRITAIN	ABROAD
1606 The Union Flag adopted as the national flag	
	1607 Jamestown founded
1609 Rebellion in Ireland	**1609** Galileo perfects his telescope
1611 The Authorised or King James version of the Bible:	

"In the beginning God created the Heaven and the Earth."

1616 The death of Shakespeare	
	1618 The Defenestration of Prague: The start of The 30 years War
1618 Sir Walter Raleigh executed:	

"Tis a sharp remedy but a sure one for all ills." of the axe

	1619 Slaves from Africa arrive in Virginia
1620 The Pilgrim Fathers depart for New England	
1624–30 War with Spain	**1624** Frans Hals's 'Laughing Cavalier'

The Reign of Charles I
1625 – 49

1626–9 War with France	**1626** New Amsterdam (New York) established by the Dutch
1628 Harvey explains the circulation of blood	**1628** The Huguenots at La Rochelle surrender to Cardinal Richelieu
1628 The Petition of Right	
1629 Parliament dissolved by King Charles	
1632 Van Dyck Painter-in-Ordinary	**1632–1653** Shah Jahan builds the Taj Mahal
1635 Rubens completes the ceiling of the Banqueting House in Whitehall	**1635** The Académie Française founded

BRITAIN	ABROAD

1636 Harvard University founded
1637 The Tulip Crash in Holland

1638 The Scots revolt over attempt
to impose Laudian Liturgy
1640–1660 The Long Parliament
1641 The Grand Remonstrance

1642 Tasmania discovered

1642 The attempted arrest of the
Five Members of Parliament:

"I have neither eyes to see nor tongue to speak in this place
but as the House is pleased to direct me." Speaker Lenthall
"I see the birds have flown." King Charles

1642 Outbreak of Civil War

1642 Montreal founded by the French
1642 Rembrandt's 'Night Watch'

1642 The Battle of Edgehill:

"Your King is your Cause, your Quarrel and your Captain." King Charles
"O Lord thou knowest how busy I must be this day.
If I forget thee, do not forget me."
Sir Jacob Astley's prayer on the morning of battle.

1643 Louis XIV becomes King of
France

1643 Thomas Browne's
'Religio Medici'

1644 The Manchus take Peking: The
Ch'ing Dynasty established

1644 The Battle of Marston Moor:

"God made them as stubble to our swords." Oliver Cromwell

1645 The Battle of Naseby
1647 The Putney Debates:

"The poorest he that is in England hath a life to live as the greatest he."
Colonel Thomas Rainborough MP

1648 Fox founds The Society of
Friends (The Quakers)

Britain	*Abroad*

1648 The Battle of Preston

1649 King Charles executed:

1648 The Peace of Westphalia ends
The 30 Years War
1649 Russian peasants made serfs

"A Subject and A Soveraign are clean different things." **King Charles**
"Rebellion to tyrants is obedience to God." **Judge Bradshaw**
"The people, under God, are the source of all just power."
The Rump Parliament

THE COMMONWEALTH
1649 – 60

1649–1650 Cromwell's conquest of
Ireland:

"I beseech you, in the bowels of Christ, think it
possible you may be mistaken."
Cromwell to the Kirk of Scotland, 1650

1650–1652 Cromwell's conquest of
Scotland
1651 The Battle of Worcester
1652 Tea arrives in Britain
1653 Cromwell proclaimed Lord
Protector:

"You have sat too long here for any good you have been doing.
Depart, I say, and let us have done with you!
In the name of God, go!"
Oliver Cromwell to Parliament
"Take away that fool's bauble!"
Of the parliamentary mace

1656 The Jews invited to return
1660 The Restoration

1656 Velazquez's 'Las Meninas'

The Reign of Charles II
1660 – 85

"I am weary of travelling and resolved to go abroad no more."

1660 The Royal Society founded
1662 The Book of Common Prayer

1664 The Ottoman Turks take
Hungary

1664–1665 The Last Great Plague:

"Bring out your dead"

1666 The Great Fire of London
1667 The Dutch in the Medway
1667 Milton's 'Paradise Lost':

"Of man's first disobedience, and the fruit of that forbidden tree whose
mortal taste brought death into the world and all our woe,
with loss of Eden."

1674 Peace with the Dutch

1674 The Poles elect Jan Sobiewski as
King
1677 Racine's 'Phèdre'

1677 John Bunyan's 'Pilgrim's
Progress':

"As I walked through the wilderness of this world…"

1679 The Habeas Corpus Act passed:
forcing the State to justify an
individual's arrest with a recognised
criminal offence and produce them
in person before a magistrate
within two days

1679 The last Dodo killed

1683 The Ottoman Turks lay siege to
Vienna
1685 The Revocation of the Edict of
Nantes

The Reign of James II
1685 – 9

1685 The Battle of Sedgemoor,
crushes Monmouth's rebellion.
Followed by the Bloody Assizes
1687 Isaac Newton's 'Principia
Mathematica'
1688 The Glorious Revolution

The Reign of William III & Mary II
1689 – 1702

"There is one way never to see your country lost,
and that is to die in the last ditch!"
King William

1689 The Bill of Rights
1690 John Locke's 'An Essay
concerning Human Understanding':

"No man's knowledge can go beyond his experience."

1690 The Battle of the Boyne:
King William defeats King James
1692 Edward Lloyd opens his coffee
shop: favoured by those involved
in insurance
1692 The Massacre of Glencoe: **1692** Christians granted official
Macdonalds massacred by   tolerance in China
Campbells
1694 The Bank of England founded
1698 Thomas Savery patents his   **1698** Goose stepping introduced in the
mine pump   Prussian army
1700 Scotland bankrupted by the
colonisation of Darien fiasco
1701 The Act of Settlement: Bars
Catholics from the throne and settles
on an appropriate Protestant
successor to the crown

BRITAIN	ABROAD

1701–13 The War of Spanish Succession
1701 Jethro Tull invents the Seed Drill

The Reign of Anne
1702 – 14

1703 St Petersburg founded by Peter the Great

1704 Gibraltar captured
1704 The Battle of Blenheim: The Duke of Malborough thwarts Louis XIV's hopes of dominating Europe
1707 The Union of England and Scotland
1710 St Paul's Cathedral completed
1712 Thomas Newcomen develops the piston engine
1713 The Treaty of Utrecht

THE HOUSE OF HANOVER

The Reign of George I 1714 – 27

1714 Gabriel Fahrenheit makes the first mercury thermometer
1715 Louis XIV dies

1715 The First Jacobite Rebellion
1720 The Collapse of the South Sea Bubble:

"An undertaking of great advantage, but nobody to know what it is."
Company prospectus of the South Sea Bubble

1721 Sir Robert Walpole becomes First or 'Prime' Minister
1725 Swift's 'Gulliver's Travels'

1725 Vivaldi's 'Four Seasons'

Reign of George II
1727 – 60

BRITAIN	ABROAD
1729 Wesley founds the Methodist Society	
1733 John Kay patents faster shuttle looms	
1735 Hogarth's 'Rake's Progress'	
1739 The War of Jenkins Ear	
1740–8 The War of Austrian Succession	
1741 Richardson's 'Pamela'	**1741** Frederick the Great beats the Austrians
1742 Handel's 'Messiah'	
1743 The Battle of Dettingen:Victory over the French. The last time a British King led his troops into battle	
1745 Jacobite rebellion under 'Bonnie' Prince Charlie	
1746 The Battle of Culloden: The Jacobites crushed	
1748 William Cullen demonstrates Refrigeration	
1749 Fielding's 'Tom Jones'	
1755 Dr Johnson's Dictionary:	**1755** The Lisbon Earthquake

"Lexicographer: A writer of dictionaries. A harmless drudge."

1756 The Black Hole of Calcutta	
1756–63 The Seven years War	
1757 Robert Clive wins the Battle of Plassey:	

"A great prince was dependent on my pleasure, an opulent city lay at my
mercy; its richest bankers bid against each other for my smiles;
I walked through vaults which were thrown open to me alone,
piled on either hand with gold and jewels!
Mr Chairman, at this moment I stand astonished at my own moderation."

1759 James Wolfe captures Quebec

The Reign of George III
1760 – 1820

"Born and educated in this country, I glory in the name of Briton."
King George

1761 The Bridgewater Canal built
1763 The Peace of Paris ends the
Seven Years War: Britain gains India
and Canada
1764 The Spinning Jenny invented
1765 Colonial Stamp Duty
1766–8 William Pitt the Elder, 'The
Great Commoner', Prime Minister:

"The poorest man may in his cottage bid defiance to all
the forces of the Crown."

1767–1776 The Royal Crescent, Bath
built
1768 Sir Joshua Reynolds becomes
the first President of the Royal
Academy
1769 Watt's steam engine:

"I sell here, Sir, what all the world desires to have—power!"
Mathew Boulton of the Watt Boulton Steam Factory

1770 Gainsborough's 'The Blue Boy'
1770 Botany Bay discovered by
Captain Cook

Britain	Abroad
1772 Lord Mansfield's Judgement: Slavery is illegal in England **1773** The Boston Tea Party **1775** The first Maratha War **1775** The Rotary Action Engine adopted by Arkwright **1775–81** The War of American Independence **1776** The American Declaration of Independence:	

> "We hold these truths to be self evident, that all men are created equal:
> That they are endowed by their Creator with certain unalienable rights;
> that among these are life, liberty, and the pursuit of happiness."

Britain	Abroad
1776 Gibbon's 'Decline & Fall of the Roman Empire' **1776** Smith's 'Wealth of Nations' **1780** The first Derby **1781** British Surrender at Yorktown **1783–1801** William Pitt the Younger, Prime Minister, Tory **1785** The first power loom **1786** The Impeachment of Warren Hastings **1787** The Kingdom of Ireland granted autonomy **1788** Penal Colony established at Botany Bay **1793–1802** War with France **1795** The Speenhamland Poor Relief System **1796** Vaccination against Smallpox **1798** Insurrection of the United Irishmen **1798** The Battle of the Nile: Nelson destroys the French Fleet, stranding Napoleon in Egypt	 **1786** Mozart's 'Marriage of Figaro' **1789** George Washington becomes the first President of the USA **1789** The French Revolution **1796** Bonaparte's Italian Campaign **1798** Haydn's 'Creation'

BRITAIN	ABROAD
1798 Malthus' 'Essay on Population'	
1801 The Act of Union, creating the United Kingdom of Great Britain and Ireland	
1801 Nelson destroys the Danish Fleet at Copenhagen	
1802–03 The Second Maratha War	
1803 The Battle of Assaye: Wellington crushes the Marathas	
1803–15 War with France	
1804–6 William Pitt, the Younger, Prime Minister, Tory	

"England has saved herself by her exertions, and will, as I trust, save Europe by her example."

BRITAIN	ABROAD
1804–6 Coalition of 'All the talents'	**1804** Beethoven's 'Eroica Symphony'
1804 Richard Trevithick's self propelled engine	**1804** Napoleon crowns himself Emperor
1805 Wordworth's 'Prelude'	
1805 The Battle of Trafalgar:	

"England expects that every man will do his duty." Nelson

BRITAIN	ABROAD
1807 The Abolition of the SlaveTrade	
1808–14 The Peninsula War	**1808** Goethe's 'Faust'
1811 The Luddites attack machinery	
1812–14 War with the US	**1812** Napoleon's army retreats from Moscow
1813 Jane Austen's 'Pride & Prejudice':	

"It is a truth universally acknowledged, that a single man in possession of a good fortune, must be in want of a wife."

BRITAIN	ABROAD
	1813 Napoleon beaten at Leipzig
	1813 Mexico declares independence
	1815 Brazil declares independence
1815 The Battle of Waterloo:	

"Ours is composed of the scum of the earth—the mere scum of the earth."
The Duke of Wellington on his army.

"Up guards and at 'em!"
The Duke of Wellington at Waterloo.
"Next to a battle lost, the greatest misery is a battle gained."
The Duke of Wellington after the Battle of Waterloo.

1818 Chile declares independence

1819 The Peterloo massacre
1819–1824 Byron's 'Don Juan'

The Reign of George IV
1820 – 30

1820 John Keats' 'Ode to Autumn':

"Season of mists and mellow fruitfullness, close bosom
friend of the maturing sun."

1820 The Cato Street conspiracy
1821 Constable's 'Hay Wain'   *1821* Peru declares independence
1822 The death of Castlereagh
1825 Trade Unions legalised
1825 The Stockton and Darlington
Railway
                                       1828 The death of Schubert

1829 Catholic Emancipation
1829 Sir Robert Peel creates the
civilian Metropolitan Police Force
1829 Stephenson's Rocket

The Reign of William IV
1830 – 37

1830 Liverpool and Manchester   *1830* Revolution in Paris
Railway
1830's Charles Babbage's Analytical   *1830* The death of Simon Bolivar
Engine
1831 Faraday discovers electrical   *1831* Belgium independent
induction

BRITAIN	ABROAD
1831 James Ross reaches magnetic North	
1832 The Great Reform Bill	**1832** Greece Independent
1833 The Factory Act bans the employment of children under nine	
1833 The launch of the Oxford Movement	
1833 Slavery abolished in the British Empire	
1834 The Transportation of the Tolpuddle Martyrs	
1836 Dickens' 'Pickwick Papers'	**1836** The Great Trek
1836 The launch of the Chartist movement	**1836** The Battle of The Alamo

The Reign of Queen Victoria 1837 – 1901

1837 The first Telegraphic message	
1838 Morse Code invented	
1838 The Anti-Corn Law league	
1838–1842 The First Afghan War	
1839 The first Grand National	
1840 The first British Colonists arrive in New Zealand	
1840 The Penny Post	
1842 The First Opium War (Britain gains Hong Kong)	
1843 Charles Napier takes Sind:	

"Peccavi!" (I have sinned)

1844 Turner's 'Rain, Steam and Speed!'	**1844** French War in Morocco
1845–6 The Great Irish Potato Famine	
1846 Repeal of the Corn Laws	
1847 Thackeray's 'Vanity Fair'	**1847** Liberia Independent
1848 The end of the Chartist Movement	**1848** Marx, Engels, 'Communist Manifesto'
	1848 The 'Year of Revolutions' in Europe
1848 Mill's 'Principles of Political Economy'	

BRITAIN	*ABROAD*

1849 Victory over the Sikhs and
conquest of the Punjab

1850–65 The Taiping Rebellion in
China
1851 Verdi's 'Rigoletto'

1851 The Great Exhibition:

"These, England's triumphs, are the trophies of a bloodless war." **Thackeray**

1851 Melville's 'Moby Dick'
1852 Napoleon III becomes Emperor

1853 Sir George Cayley's coachman
achieves the first manned glider flight
1854–56 The Crimean War:
1854 The Charge of the Light
Brigade at Balaclava. The sick
tended by Florence Nightingale,
The Lady of the Lamp:

"The very first requirement in a Hospital is that
it should do the sick no harm!"

1855–58 Henry Temple, Viscount
Palmerston, Prime Minister, Liberal:

"As the Roman, in days of old, held himself free from indignity,
when he could say Civis Romanus sum; so also a British Subject,
in whatever land he may be, shall feel confident that the watchful eye and
the strong arm of England will protect him against injustice and wrong."

1855 Trollope's 'The Warden'

1856 Flaubert's 'Madame Bovary'

1857 Civil Divorce becomes possible
1857 The Opium War
1857–8 The Indian Mutiny
1858 The East India Company
abolished
1859–65 Henry Temple, Viscount
Palmerston, Prime Minister, Liberal
1859 Darwin's 'Origin of Species':

"I have called this principle, by which each slight variation, if useful, is preserved, by the term of Natural Selection."

BRITAIN	ABROAD
1860 Barry's Houses of Parliament open	*1860* Victor Emmanuel proclaimed King of Italy by Garibaldi *1861* Tsar Alexander II liberates the Serfs *1861–1865* The American Civil War *1862* Doctor Gatling invents his machine gun, 'The Gatling Gun' *1864* Pasteurisation invented by Pasteur *1864* The International Red Cross founded in Switzerland *1865* Lincoln shot *1866* Alfred Nobel invents dynamite
1867 Canada established as the first Dominion *1867* Fenian insurrection in Ireland *1868–74* William Gladstone, Prime Minister, Liberal *1868–1869* Browning's 'The Ring & The Book' *1870* Forster's Education Act; Civil Service Exams	*1867* The typewriter invented *1867* Marx's 'Das Kapital' *1869* The Suez Canal completed *1870* The Franco Prussian War *1871–90* Bismarck becomes the first Chancellor of the newly united Germany
1872 Henry Stanley finds David Livingstone:	

"Dr Livingstone, I presume?"

BRITAIN	ABROAD
1872 George Eliot's 'Middlemarch' *1874–80* Benjamin Disraeli, Prime Minister, Conservative *1874* Hardy's 'Far from the Madding Crowd' *1875* The first Gilbert and Sullivan operetta	*1872* Tolstoy's 'Anna Karenina' *1874* The first Impressionist Exhibition

BRITAIN	ABROAD
	1876 Wagner's 'Ring Cycle'
	1876 Alexander Graham Bell invents the telephone
1877 The Proclamation of the Empire of India	
1879 The Zulu War	
	1879 Edison demonstrates his electric light
1880–85 William Gladstone, Prime Minister, Liberal	
1880 The First Boer War	
1880 W.G. Grace scores first ever test century against Australia	
1882 The Occupation of Egypt	*1882* Daimler invents the petrol engine
1885 Gordon killed at Khartoum	*1885* Karl Benz builds the first petrol fuelled car
1886 Burma conquered	
1886 First Irish Home Rule Bill defeated	
1888 Kipling's 'Plain Tales from the Hills'	*1888* Van Gogh's 'Sunflowers'
1889 Cecil Rhodes establishes the British South Africa Company:	

"Remember that you are an Englishman,
and have consequently won first prize in the lottery of life."

BRITAIN	ABROAD
1893 Second Irish Home Rule Bill —rejected by Lords	
	1894 The Dreyfus case
1895 The Jameson raid	
1895 Marconi transmits his Wireless messages	
1896 The conquest of Sudan	*1896* The first Modern Olympics
1896 The first cinema (in Leicester Square)	
1898 The Battle of Omdurman	*1898* The Spanish American War
	1898 The Curies discover radium
1899–1902 The Second Boer War	
1899 Elgar's 'Enigma Variations'	
1900 The Labour Party founded	*1900* The Boxer Rebellion

BRITAIN	*ABROAD*

1901 Australia becomes the first self-governing member of the British Empire

THE HOUSE OF SAXE – COBURG – GOTHA
The Reign of Edward VII
1901 – 10

1902–5 Arthur Balfour, Prime Minister, Conservative

1904 The Anglo French Entente Cordiale

1905–8 Sir Henry Campbell-Bannerman, Prime Minister, Liberal
1907 Signing of the Triple Entente
1908–16 H.H. Asquith, Prime Minister, Liberal
1909 Employment Exchanges Introduced

1903 The Wright Brothers achieve the first manned, powered flight
1904 Freud's 'Psychopathology of Everyday Life'
1905 The Russian Japanese War
1905 Einsteins's theory of relativity

THE HOUSE OF WINDSOR
The Reign of George V
1910 – 1936

1911 The Delhi Durbar
1911 The First National Health Insurance Bill
1911 The House of Lords veto abolished
1912 Captain Scott's Last Expedition:

"I am just going outside and may be sometime." Captain Oates

1912 Passage of Irish Home Rule Bill
1913 Charlie Chaplin appears in his first film

| *BRITAIN* | *ABROAD* |

1914 – 1918 THE FIRST WORLD WAR

"Their name liveth for ever more." The Stone of Sacrifice

1914 The British Expeditionary Force
sent to defend Belgium
1915 Brooke's 'The Soldier':

"If I should die, think only this of me: That there's some corner of a foreign
field that is forever England."

1916–22 David Lloyd George, Prime
Minister, Liberal
1916 Conscription introduced
1916 The Battle of the Somme
1916 The Battle of Jutland
1916 The Easter Rising in Dublin
1917 The Battle of Passchendaele   *1917* US troops arrive in France
    1917 The Russian Revolution

"What is our task? To make Britain a fit country for Heroes to live in."
Lloyd George

1918 11am November 11ᵗʰ. The Armistice. The end of The Great War.

1918 Votes for all men over 21 and
women over 30
1919 The Treaty of Versailles   *1919* The League of Nations
1919–20 The Anglo-Irish War
1920 Ulster secedes from Ireland   *1920–33* Prohibition in USA
1921 Rutherford & Chadwick split
the atom
1922–23 Bonar Law, Prime Minister,
Conservative
1922 Eliot's 'The Wasteland'   *1922* Mussolini Marches on Rome
1922 Joyces's 'Ulysses'
1922 The Anglo-Irish Treaty:
Partition of Ireland
1922–3 The Irish Civil War

1923–4 Stanley Baldwin, Prime
Minister, Conservative
1924 Ramsay MacDonald, Prime
Minister, Labour   **1924** The Death of Lenin
1924–29 Stanley Baldwin, Prime   **1924** Stalin takes power
Minister, Conservative
1925 Return to the Gold Standard
1926 The General Strike
1926 Baird invents television
1928 Lawrence's 'Lady Chatterly's
Lover' and Waugh's 'Decline and Fall'
1928 Sir Alexander Fleming
discovers penicillin
1929 Votes for Women over 21   **1929** The Wall Street Crash
1929 The BBC begins television
broadcasting
1929–35 Ramsay Macdonald, Prime   **1929** Hemingway's 'A Farewell to
Minister, Labour   Arms'
1930 Mohandas (the Mahatma)
Gandhi leads the Salt March in India
1931 National Government led by
Ramsay Macdonald
1931 British Dominions made
Independent
1931 The Gold Standard Abandoned   **1931** The Japanese invade Manchuria
    1933 Hitler becomes Chancellor of
    Germany

1935–7 Stanley Baldwin, Prime
Minister, Conservative
1935 Watson Watt devises radar   **1936** Italy Annexes Abyssinia
1936 Keynes' 'General theory of   **1936–9** The Spanish Civil War
Employment, Interest and Money'
1936 Edward VIII Abdicates:

"Our cock won't fight." Beaverbrook to Churchill

The Reign of George VI
1936 – 52

    1936 Picasso's 'Guernica'

BRITAIN	ABROAD

BRITAIN   **ABROAD**

1937 Whittle invents the jet engine
1937–40 Neville Chamberlain,   **1937** The Irish Free State becomes Eire
Prime Minister, Conservative
1938 Chamberlain with Hitler at
Munich:

"I believe it is peace for our time."

1939 – 1945 THE SECOND WORLD WAR

"When you go home, tell them of us and say, for your tomorrow
we gave our today."

1940–5 Winston Churchill, Prime
Minister, Conservative:

"I have nothing to offer but blood, toil, tears and sweat."

1940 Dunkirk:

"Let us therefore brace ourselves to our duties, and so bear ourselves that, if
the British Empire and its Commonwealth last for a thousand years,
men will still say, 'This was their finest hour.'" Churchill

1940 The Battle of Britain:

"Never in the field of human conflict was so much owed by
so many to so few." Churchill

BRITAIN	ABROAD
	1941 Pearl Harbour
	1942 The Wannsee Conference
1942 The Beveridge Report	discusses 'The Jewish Question' and
1942 The Fall of Singapore	decides on 'The Final Solution', the
1942 The Battle of El Alamein	extermination of all European Jews: The
	Holocaust
1943 The Allies invade Italy	**1943** Germans surrender in N. Africa
1944 D-Day: The invasion of France	and Stalingrad
1944 The Battle of Imphal	**1944** The Liberation of Paris
	1945 The Yalta Conference
	1945 The United Nations established
	1945 Atomic Bombs dropped on
	Nagasaki and Hiroshima

BRITAIN	ABROAD
1945–51 Clement Atlee, Prime Minister, Labour: Nationalisation begins **1946** The National Health Service	

"An iron curtain has descended across the continent."
(Europe) Churchill 1946

BRITAIN	ABROAD
	1947 The Americans exceed the spee[of sound **1947** India, Pakistan and Burma gain Independence
1948 West Indian immigrants arrive on the SS Empire Windrush	**1948** The Jewish National Council proclaims the new State of Israel **1949** The Berlin Airlift
1949 Orwell's '1984'	**1949** The Peoples Republic of China established **1949** Eire becomes the Irish Republic and leaves the Commonwealth **1949** Nato founded **1950–3** The Korean War
1951–55 Winston Churchill, Prime Minister, Conservative	

The Reign of Queen Elizabeth II
1952 – Present

BRITAIN	ABROAD
1953 Francis Crick and JamesWatson identify the structure of DNA **1954** Tolkien's 'Lord of the Rings' **1954** Rationing ends **1955–7** Sir Anthony Eden, Prime Minister, Conservative **1956** The Suez Crisis	**1953** The Death of Stalin
1956 Osborne's 'Look Back in Anger' **1956** Nuclear Power Station Calder Hall opens	**1956** The Soviet invasion of Hungary
1957–63 Harold Macmillan, Prime Minister, Conservative	**1957** Ghana gains independence

BRITAIN	ABROAD
	1957 The Treaty of Rome: The EEC founded
	1958 De Gaulle President of France
1959 The first Motorway, the M1, opened	
1960 National Service ends	*1960* Nigeria gains independence

"The wind of change is blowing through the continent."
(Africa) Macmillan 1960

BRITAIN	ABROAD
1962 The Beatles reach No 1	*1962* The Cuban Missile Crisis
1963–4 Sir Alec Douglas-Home, Prime Minister, Conservative	*1963* Kennedy shot
	1963–75 War in Vietnam
1964–70 Harold Wilson, Prime Minister, Labour	
1965 Rhodesia makes the Unilateral Declaration of Independence, UDI	
1965 Capital Punishment abandoned	
1966 England wins the World Cup	*1966* The Cultural Revolution enforced in China
1967 Homosexual Acts and Abortion legalised	*1967* The Six Day War between Israel and Egypt
1968 Civil 'Troubles' begin in Northern Ireland	*1968* The Russian invasion of Czechoslovakia
1969 Indians forced out of Uganda and Kenya flee to Britain	
1969 North Sea oil discovered	*1969* The first Man steps on the Moon
1969 The Divorce Act becomes effective	
1970–4 Edward Heath, Prime Minister, Conservative	
1972 Bloody Sunday. Devolved Government in Northern Ireland suspended	
1973 The UK joins the European Common Market	*1973* The Americans leave Vietnam
	1973 The Yom Kippur War
1974–6 Harold Wilson, Prime Minister, Labour	

BRITAIN	ABROAD
1976–9 Jim Callaghan, PrimeMinister, Labour	
1979 Failed British Referenda on Devolution for Wales and Scotland	**1979** Ronald Reagan elected President of the U.S.A.
1979 The Winter of Discontent	**1979** War in Afghanistan
1979–90 Margaret Thatcher, Prime Minister, Conservative: Privatisation begins	
1980 Majority rule in Rhodesia	**1980–8** The Iran-Iraq War
1982 The Falklands War	
1984 The Miners' Strike	
	1985 Gorbachev comes to power in USSR
1986 The Single European Act	**1986** The US bombs Libya
	1989 Solidarity takes power in Poland
	1989 The Tiananmen Square Massacre
1990 John Major, Prime Minister, Conservative	**1989** The Berlin Wall torn down
1991 Britain signs the Maastricht Treaty	
1991 The First Gulf War	
1991 Sir Tim Berners Lee invents the World Wide Web	
1992 Britain leaves the European Exchange Rate Mechanism	
1997 (– present) Tony Blair, Prime Minister, Labour	**1993–5** War in Yugoslavia
1997 The death of Diana, Princess of Wales	**1994** The End of Apartheid
	1997 Hong Kong surrendered to The People's Republic of China
1998 The Good Friday Agreement	
1999 Devolution for Wales and Scotland	
	1999 The Euro launched
2003 The Second Gulf War	**2001** '9/11' Al Qaeda destroy the World Trade Centre
2003 England Wins the Rugby World Cup	

SPEECHES, COMMANDMENTS AND CHARTERS

THE TEN COMMANDMENTS
Exodus 20 The King James Bible

And God spake all these words, saying, I am the Lord thy God, which have brought thee out of the land of Egypt, out of the house of bondage.

Thou shalt have no other gods before me.

Thou shalt not make unto thee any graven image, or any likeness of any thing that is in heaven above, or that is in the earth beneath, or that is in the water under the earth:

Thou shalt not bow down thyself to them, nor serve them: for I the Lord thy God am a jealous God, visiting the iniquity of the fathers upon the children unto the third and fourth generation of them that hate me; And shewing mercy unto thousands of them that love me, and keep my commandments.

Thou shalt not take the name of the Lord thy God in vain; for the Lord will not hold him guiltless that taketh his name in vain.

Remember the sabbath day, to keep it holy. Six days shalt thou labour, and do all thy work: But the seventh day is the sabbath of the Lord thy God: in it thou shalt not do any work, thou, nor thy son, nor thy daughter, thy manservant, nor thy maidservant, nor thy cattle, nor thy stranger that is within thy gates: For in six days the Lord made heaven and earth, the sea, and all that in them is, and rested the seventh day: wherefore the Lord blessed the sabbath day, and hallowed it.

Honour thy father and thy mother: that thy days may be long upon the land which the Lord thy God giveth thee.

Thou shalt not kill.

Thou shalt not commit adultery.

Thou shalt not steal.

Thou shalt not bear false witness against thy neighbour.

Thou shalt not covet thy neighbour's house, thou shalt not covet thy neighbour's wife, nor his manservant, nor his maidservant, nor his ox, nor his ass, nor any thing that is thy neighbour's.

JESUS
The Great Commandment
Matthew 22 The King James Bible

Thou shalt love the Lord thy God with all thy heart, and with all thy soul, and with all thy mind.
This is the first and great Commandment.
And the second is like unto it, Thou shalt love thy neighbour as thyself.
On these two commandments hang all the law and the prophets.

JESUS
From The Sermon on the Mount
MATTHEW 6 The King James Bible

"After this manner therefore pray ye:

Our Father which art in heaven,
Hallowed be thy name.
Thy kingdom come.
Thy will be done in earth,
as it is in heaven.
Give us this day our daily bread.
And forgive us our debts,
as we forgive our debtors.
And lead us not into temptation,
but deliver us from evil:
For thine is the kingdom,
and the power, and the glory, for ever. Amen."

From the "Ecclesiastical History of the English People" by the Venerable Bede
The speech by one of King Edwin of Northumbria's Saxon Noblemen in favour of Christianity.

Such seemeth to me, my lord the present life of men here on earth…as if a sparrow should come to the house and very swiftly flit through…which entereth in at one window and straightaway passeth out through another while you sit at dinner with your captains and servants in wintertime; the parlour being then made warm with the fire kindled in the midst thereof, but all places being troubled with raging tempests of winter rain and snow. Right for the time it be within the house it feeleth no smart of the winter storm but after a very short space of fair weather it soon passeth again from winter to winter and escapeth your sight. So the life of man here appeareth for a little season, but what followeth or what hath gone before that surely we know not. Wherefore if this new learning hath brought us any better surety, methinks it is worthy to be followed.

THE MAGNA CARTA
The Great Charter of liberties extorted from King John by his Barons in 1215

Clause 39:
No free man shall be taken or imprisoned or dispossessed, or outlawed or exiled, or in any way destroyed, nor will we go upon him, nor will we send against him except by the lawful judgement of his peers or by the law of the land.

Clause 40:
To no man will we sell, or deny, or delay, right or Justice.

ENGLAND
Act II Scene I, "Richard II" by William Shakespeare

This royal throne of kings, this scepter'd isle,
This earth of majesty, this seat of Mars,
This other Eden, demi-paradise,
This fortress built by Nature for herself
Against infection and the hand of war,
This happy breed of men, this little world,
This precious stone set in the silver sea,
Which serves it in the office of a wall,
Or as a moat defensive to a house,
Against the envy of less happier lands,
This blessed plot, this earth, this realm, this
England,
This nurse, this teeming womb of royal kings,
Fear'd by their breed and famous by their birth,
Renowned for their deeds…. Far from home, -
For Christian service and true chivalry, -

THE FEAST OF CRISPIAN
Act IV Scene III, "Henry V" by William Shakespeare

This day is call'd the feast of Crispian:
He that outlives this day, and comes safe home,
Will stand a tip-toe when this day is nam'd,
And rouse him at the name of Crispian.
He that shall live this day, and see old age,
Will yearly on the vigil feast his neighbours,
And say, "To-morrow is Saint Crispian":
Then will he strip his sleeve and show his scars,
And say, "These wounds I had on Crispin's day".
Old men forget: yet all shall be forgot,
But he'll remember with advantages
What feats he did that day. Then shall our names,
Familiar in his mouth as household words,
Harry the king, Bedford and Exeter,
Warwick and Talbot, Salisbury and Gloucester,
Be in their flowing cups freshly remember'd.
This story shall the good man teach his son;
And Crispin Crispian shall ne'er go by,
From this day to the ending of the world,
But we in it shall be remembered;
We few, we happy few, we band of brothers;
For he to-day that sheds his blood with me
Shall be my brother; be he ne'er so vile
This day shall gentle his condition:
And gentlemen in England, now a-bed
Shall think themselves accurs'd they were not here,
And hold their manhoods cheap whiles any speaks
That fought with us upon Saint Crispin's day.

ELIZABETH I
Addressing her troops at Tilbury while awaiting the arrival of the Spanish Armada in 1588

My loving people, We have been persuaded by some that are careful of our safety to take heed how we commit ourselves to armed multitudes for fear of treachery, but I assure you I do not desire to live to distrust my faithful and loving people. Let Tyrants fear; I have always so behaved myself under God, I have placed my chiefest strength and safeguard in the loyal hearts and goodwill of my subjects. And therefore I am come amongst you, as you see, at this time not for my recreation and disport, but being resolved in the midst and heat of battle to live and die amongst you all. To lay down for God, my kingdom and for my people, my honour and my blood even in the dust. I know I have the body of a weak and feeble woman, but I have the heart and stomach of a King and a King of England too and think it foul scorn that Parma or Spain or any Prince of Europe should dare to invade the borders of my realm; to which, rather than any dishonour shall grow by me, I myself will take up arms, I myself will be your General, Judge and Rewarder of every one of your virtues in the field. I know already for your forwardness you have deserved rewards and crowns, and we do assure you, on the word of a Prince, they shall be duly paid you.

CHARLES I
From the scaffold before his execution in 1649

'I never did begin a War with the two Houses of Parliament, and I call God to witness, to whom I must shortly make an account, That I never did intend for to incroach upon their Privileges, they began upon me.'

'For the People ... truly I desire their Liberty and Freedom as much as any body whomsoever; but I must tell you, That their Liberty and Freedom consist in having of Government, those Laws, by which their Life and their Goods may be most their own. It is not for having share in Government (Sir) that is nothing pertaining to them. A Subject and a Soveraign are clean different things.'

'I go from a corruptible to an incorruptible Crown; where no disturbance can be, no disturbance in the world.'

SATAN
From "Paradise Lost" by John Milton

What though the field be lost?
All is not lost; the unconquerable Will,
And study of revenge, immortal hate,
And courage never to submit or yield:
And what is else not to be overcome?
That Glory never shall his wrath or might
Extort from me. To bow and sue for grace
With suppliant knee, and deifie his power
Who from the terrour of this Arm so late
Doubted his Empire, that were low indeed,
That were an ignominy and shame beneath
This downfall; since by Fate the strength of Gods
And this Empyreal substance cannot fail,
Since through experience of this great event
In Arms not worse, in foresight much advancît,
We may with more successful hope resolve
To wage by force or guile eternal Warr
Irreconcileable, to our grand Foe,
Who now triumphs, and in th'excess of joy
Sole reigning holdst the Tyranny of Heav'n.

WINSTON CHURCHILL
Speech in the House of Commons 13 May 1940

I would say to the House, as I said to those who have joined this Government "I have nothing to offer but blood, toil, tears and sweat." We have before us an ordeal of the most grievous kind. We have before us many, many long months of struggle and of suffering. You ask what is our policy? I will say: It is to wage war, by sea, land and air, with all our might and with all the strength that God can give us; to wage war against a monstrous tyranny, never surpassed in the dark, lamentable catalogue of human crime. That is our policy. You ask, What is our aim? I answer in one word: Victory-victory at all costs, victory in spite of all terror, victory, however long and hard the road may be; for without victory there is no survival. Let that be realised; no survival for the British Empire; no survival for all that the British Empire has stood for, no survival for the urge and impulse of the ages, that mankind will move forward towards its goal. But I take up my task with buoyancy and hope. I feel sure that our cause will not be suffered to fail among men. At this time I feel entitled to claim the aid of all and I say, "Come, then, let us go forward together with our united strength."

WINSTON CHURCHILL
Speech in the House of Commons, 4 June 1940

We shall not flag or fail. We shall go on to the end. We shall fight in France, we shall fight on the seas and oceans, we shall fight with growing confidence and growing strength in the air, we shall defend our island, whatever the cost may be. We shall fight on the beaches, we shall fight on the landing grounds, we shall fight in the fields and in the streets, we shall fight in the hills; we shall never surrender.

WINSTON CHURCHILL
Speech in the House of Commons 18 June 1940

What General Weygand called the Battle of France is over. I expect that the battle of Britain is about to begin. Upon this battle depends the survival of Christian civilisation. Upon it depends our own British life, and the long continuity of our institutions and our Empire. The whole fury and might of the enemy must very soon be turned on us. Hitler knows that he will have to break us in this island or lose the war. If we can stand up to him, all Europe may be free and the life of the world may move forward into broad, sunlit uplands. But if we fail, then the whole world, including the United States, including all that we have known and cared for, will sink into the abyss of a new dark age made more sinister, and perhaps more protracted, by the lights of perverted science. Let us therefore brace ourselves to our duties, and so bear ourselves that, if the British Empire and its Commonwealth last for a thousand years, men will still say, "This was their finest hour."

SONGS

THE 23rd PSALM
The King James Bible

The Lord is my shepherd: I shall not want.
He maketh me to lie down in green pastures: he leadeth me beside the still waters.
He restoreth my soul: He leadeth me in the paths of righteousness for his name's sake.
Yea, though I walk through the valley of the shadow of death, I will fear no evil: for thou art with me; thy rod and thy staff they comfort me.
Thou preparest a table before me in the presence of mine enemies: Thou anointest my head with oil; my cup runneth over.
Surely goodness and mercy shall follow me all the days of my life: and I will dwell in the house of the Lord for ever.

"GOD SAVE THE KING" (1745)
Words (attributed): Henry Carey (1687–1743)
Music: Dr Thomas Arne (1710–1778)

God save our gracious King;
Long live our noble King;
God save the King!
Send him victorious,
Happy and glorious,
Long to reign over us
God save the King!

O Lord our God arise,
Scatter his enemies,
And make them fall:
Confound their politics,
Frustrate their knavish tricks,
On Thee our hopes we fix;
God save us all!

Thy choicest gifts in store
On him be pleased to pour;

Long may he reign:
May he defend our laws,
And ever give us cause
To sing with heart and voice,
God save the King!

"RULE, BRITANNIA!" (1740)
Words: James Thompson (1700–1748)
Music: Dr Thomas Arne (1710–1778)

When Britain first, at Heaven's command,
Arose from out the azure main,
This was the charter of the land,
And guardian angels sang this strain –
'Rule, Britannia! Britannia, rule the waves;
Britons never, never, never shall be slaves.'

The nations, not so blest as thee,
Must in their turns to tyrants fall,
Whilst thou shalt flourish great and free,
The dread and envy of them all.
Rule, Britannia! etc.

Still more majestic shalt thou rise,
More dreadful from each foreign stroke,
As the loud blast that tears the skies,
Serves but to root thy native oak.
Rule, Britannia! etc.

Thee haughty tyrants ne'er shall tame,
All their attempts to bend thee down,
Will but arouse thy generous flame,
And work their woe and thy renown.
Rule, Britannia! etc.

To thee belongs the rural reign,
Thy cities shall with commerce shine,

And thine shall be the subject main,
And every shore it circles thine.
Rule, Britannia! etc.

The Muses, still with freedom found,
Shall to thy happy coast repair,
Blest isle with matchless beauty crowned,
And manly hearts to guard the fair.
Rule, Britannia! etc.

"JERUSALEM" (1915)
Words: William Blake (1757–1827)
Music: Hubert Parry (1848–1918)

And did those feet in ancient times,
Walk upon England's mountains green?
And was the holy Lamb of God,
On England's pleasant pastures seen?
And did the countenance divine,
Shine forth upon our clouded hills?
And was Jerusalem builded here,
Among these dark Satanic mills?

Bring me my bow of burning gold!
Bring me my arrows of desire!
Bring me my spear! O clouds unfold!
Bring me my chariot of fire!
I will not cease from mental fight,
Nor shall my sword sleep in my hand,
Till we have built Jerusalem,
In England's green and pleasant land.

"I VOW TO THEE MY COUNTRY" (1918)
Words: Cecil Spring-Rice (1859–1918)
Music: Gustav Holst (1874–1934)

I vow to thee, my country all earthly things above,
Entire and whole and perfect, the service of my love;
The love that asks no question, the love that stands the test,
That lays upon the altar the dearest and the best;
The love that never falters, the love that pays the price,
The love that makes undaunted the final sacrifice.

And there's another country, I've heard of long ago,
Most dear to them that love her, most great to them that know;
We may not count her armies, we may not see her King,
Her fortress is a faithful heart, her pride is suffering;
And soul by soul and silently her shining bounds increase,
And her ways are ways of gentleness and all her paths are peace.

"LAND OF HOPE AND GLORY" (1897)
Words: Arthur C. Benson (1862–1925)
Music: Edward Elgar (1857–1934)

Dear Land of Hope, thy hope is crowned.
God make thee mightier yet!
On Sov'ran brows, beloved, renowned,
Once more thy crown is set.
Thine equal laws, by Freedom gained,
Have ruled thee well and long;
By Freedom gained, by Truth maintained,
Thine Empire shall be strong.

Chorus
Land of Hope and Glory,
Mother of the Free,
How shall we extol thee,
Who are born of thee?

Wider still and wider
Shall thy bounds be set;
God, who made thee mighty,
Make thee mightier yet.

Thy fame is ancient as the days,
As Ocean large and wide:
A pride that dares and heeds not praise,
A stern and silent pride:
Not that false joy that dreams content
With what our sires have won;
The blood a hero sire hath spent
Still nerves a hero son.

Chorus

THE BRITISH EMPIRE AND IMPERIAL TERRITORIES IN 1920 AND THE YEAR IN WHICH THEY CAME UNDER BRITISH CONTROL

Aden	1839	Gold Coast Colony	c1650
Alberta	c1788	Grenada	1762
Anglo-Egyptian Sudan	1899	Hong Kong	1841
Antigua	1632	Iraq	1920
Bahamas	1666	Jamaica	1655
Barbados	1605	Kenya Colony	1888
Basutoland	1868	Lagos	1861
Bechuanaland		Madras	1639
Protectorate	1885	Malta	1800
Bengal	1633	Manitoba	1811
Bermudas	1609	Mauritius	1810
Bhutan	1864	Montserrat	1632
Bombay	1608	Natal	1824
British Columbia	1821	Nevis	1628
British Honduras	1638	New Brunswick	1713
British North Borneo	1881	New South Wales	1788
British Somaliland	1884	New Zealand	1840
Brunei	1888	Newfoundland	1583
Burma	1824	Nigeria	1884
Cameroon	1919	Nova Scotia	1623
Cape Breton Island	1758	Nyasaland Protectorate	1891
Cape of Good Hope		Ontario	1759
(Cape Colony)	1795	Orange River Colony	1848
Cayman Islands	1670	Palestine	1919
Ceylon	1795	Prince Edward Island	1758
Cyprus	1878	Punjab	1849
Demerara, Berbice,		Quebec	1759
Essequibo	1796	Queensland	1824
Dominica	1761	Rhodesia	1888
Eastern Bengal & Assam	1825	Rupertís Land and North-	
Egypt	1882	West Territory	1670
Falkland Islands	1765	Sarawak	1888
Federated Malay States	1874	Saskatchewan	1766
Gambia	c1618	Seychelles	1794
Gibraltar	1704	Sierra Leone	1787
		Singapore	1819

South Australia	1836
South West Africa	1919
St Christopher (St Kitts)	1623
St Lucia	1605
St Vincent	1762
Straits Settlements	1786
Swaziland	1890
Tanganyika Territory	1919
Tasmania	1803
Tobago	1763
Togoland	1919
Transjordan	1920
Transvaal	1877
Trinidad	1797
Uganda	1890
Vancouver Island	1821
Victoria	1834
Virgin Islands	1666
Western Australia	1826
Zanzibar Protectorate	1890
Zululand	1887

IMPERIAL WEIGHTS AND MEASURES c1830

Length	Liquid Volume (Beer and Ale)
1 mile = 1,760 yards	1 tun = 2 butts
1 furlong = 220 yards	1 butt = 2 hogsheads
1 chain = 22 yards = 100 links	1 hogshead = 1 ½ barrels
1 rod, pole or perch = 5 ½ yards	1 barrel = 2 kilderkins
1 yard = 3 feet = 36 inches	1 kilderkin = 2 firkins
1 foot = 12 inches	1 firkin = 9 gallons
1 span = 9 inches	1 gallon = 4 quarts
1 hand = 4 inches	1 quart = 2 pints
1 nail = 2 ¼ inches (for cloth)	1 pint = 4 gills
1 inch = 1/36th of a yard	1 gill = 5 fluid ounces
1 fathom = 6 feet	1 fluid ounce = 8 fluid drachms
1 cable = 600 feet	1 fluid drachm = 60 minims
1 nautical mile = 6,080 feet	

Area	Dry Measure
1 square mile = 640 acres	1 chaldron = 36 bushels
1 acre = 10 sq. chains = 4 roods	1 quarter = 8 bushels
1 rood = 40 sq. poles	1 bushel = 4 pecks
1 sq. pole = 30 ¼ sq. yards	1 peck = 2 gallons
1 sq. yard = 9 sq. feet	1 gallon = 4 quarts
1 sq. foot = 144 Sq. inches	1 quart = 2 pints
	1 pint = 4 gills

Money	Weight Avoirdupois
1 guinea = 21 shillings	1 ton = 20 hundredweight (cwt)
1 pound sterling = 20 shillings	1 hundredweight = 4 quarters
1 crown = 5 shillings	1 quarter = 2 stones
1 shilling = 12 pence	1 stone = 14 pounds (lb)
1 penny = 4 farthings	1 pound = 16 ounces (oz) = 7,000 grains
	1 ounce = 16 drams = 437 ½ grains
	1 dram = 27.34 grains